IRIDESCENT

SARA TENDULKAR

Copyright © Sara Tendulkar
All Rights Reserved.

ISBN 978-1-63886-761-6

This book has been published with all efforts taken to make the material error-free after the consent of the author. However, the author and the publisher do not assume and hereby disclaim any liability to any party for any loss, damage, or disruption caused by errors or omissions, whether such errors or omissions result from negligence, accident, or any other cause.

While every effort has been made to avoid any mistake or omission, this publication is being sold on the condition and understanding that neither the author nor the publishers or printers would be liable in any manner to any person by reason of any mistake or omission in this publication or for any action taken or omitted to be taken or advice rendered or accepted on the basis of this work. For any defect in printing or binding the publishers will be liable only to replace the defective copy by another copy of this work then available.

Dedicated to all non-humans, who poke holes in the pages of a book with a pencil and scribble violently, with reckless abandon. Do that to other books, not this.

Contents

1. Nature Chose Her — 1
2. There's No Bookmark For My Daydreams — 3
3. Close To Fantasy — 7
4. Blue — 8
5. The Fire Of Holika — 10
6. Holi — 12
7. Halcyon — 14
8. Story Of Every Politician — 17
9. What Am I Related To? — 22
10. When I Said The Wrong 'happy Birthday' — 24
11. Unlock That Cage — 27
12. Hill He'd Always Wanted To Climb — 29
13. The Real Kind Of Adventures — 32
14. Work Like Crazy — 37
15. Watchout! There's Smoke Coming Out Of Your Eyes — 39
16. Wild Little Storm — 41
17. Paper Boats — 43
18. Unity — 45
19. The Sky Full Of Words — 46

1. Nature Chose Her

She opened her eyes ,
Her beautiful eyeballs,
Reflecting the dancing butterflies,
And the foamy waterfalls.

She belongs to nature,
Her body's wrapped in leaves,
Just like a beautiful architecture,
That the galaxy interweaves.

You can't keep her in a cage,
She knows how to fly,
She controls nature's stage,
And she very well knows how to find the sky.

Nature chose her,
Because she's what the trees prefer.
She attracts all the birds,
Who come singing in flocks and herds.
'Cause she waters all the plants and trees
Just by having the raindrops freeze.

The flowers blossom towards her
The dandelions fly towards her.
She dances with the wind, she sings with the birds all lined.
Just with a snap of her fingers,
She adds moonlight to the waterfalls,
And the echo of light lingers,
In her eyeballs.

-Sara Tendulkar

2. There's No Bookmark For My Daydreams

The ink from the books,
The light from the stars,
The looks of the crooks,
All crept in my head along with the avatars.

The thoughts just sat in my head to sip some tea,
And casually introduced me to the colorful sea.
They gave me a dress made of sunshine,
Which smelled of books.
Oh and on that dress of sunshine,
Were words which looked like mine,
The stories I had written,
The places I had felt,
All had been knitten
By the goblins I had met.

Words write themselves on me,
As I paint the sky ,
Glad is the sea ,
To read the stories for thee.

I can pick up the stars and make my galaxy,
There's no Newton, there's no gravity.
Every day a new story writes itself on me,
And takes me into it,
As fast as I can be.
No one can understand my eyes,
And the paintings I make on the skies.
No one knows I can shrink the universe,
And double it too along with my free verse.
No one knows how I fly to the moon,
To write stories on the craters,
Which sound like a wonderful tune.

My thoughts become more and more wild,
As I actually start smelling books without actually being near any,
And my heart synchronizes its beats with the twist of the story.

SARA TENDULKAR

My thoughts look like beautiful empty pages,
On which I can go on writing for ages.
I just have to pick a pen,
And all I do is write every now and then.
Then, I just have to pour that out on a paper,
So everyone can read what's there on my crater.

My head thinks about all the what if's,
And the thoughts keep growing wild.
Sometimes Simba falls off the cliff,
And Mufasa yells 'Oh, my child!'

Oh and in my thoughts,
All the cats do is bark,
The dogs say 'meow',
Woah, everything turns to a question mark,
As each thought stands in the long queue.

Wear the mystery, wear the songs,
Enter your story, to experience the rights and wrongs.
Thoughts inside my head,
Are vaster than the sea,
And stars reflecting on the waterbed,
Dance melodiously in my galaxy.

IRIDESCENT

My eyes open wide,
And I realize I'm not poetry,
My feelings don't have rhyme,
But my heart sure carries a story.

A bird can teach me to soar,
A lion can teach me to roar,
I can make my thoughts come true,
If I believe I have the hot glue,
To stick myself to them so hard,
That everyone will carve 'this crazy girl died lost in her thoughts '
in my graveyard.

-Sara Tendulkar

3. Close To Fantasy

That mysterious foggy evening,
Ever so pink and blue,
When I seriously wasn't dreaming,
I saw a pegasus breakthrough.

Its beautiful white wings,
And it's head with a horn,
Just like the things,
With which a book is born.

Suddenly, suddenly, it started snowing,
And that naughty little thing,
Disappeared within a blink.
I looked over the bridges and trees,
But the fog was wild pink,
But seriously, seriously I wasn't dreaming,
I tell you, all this happened on a foggy evening.
    -Sara Tendulkar

4. Blue

Color of love-
Red for you,
for me it's blue.

Blue my soul,
Blue the skies,
Which rock and roll,
With butterflies.

When you give me a brush,
And I have no clue,
I imagine that waterthrush,
And I paint all shades of blue.

Blue are my emotions,
Blue are the feelings that live inside me,
Just like vast, sparkling oceans,
Giving me vibes of what I wanna be.

SARA TENDULKAR

This color has a beautiful mystery,
It's so fantasy-like.
It shows us it's simplicity,
Just like each wave of ocean specializes in synchronicity.

Whenever I look at a rainbow,
It's the first color I see.
And ah, that beautiful glow.
Gives me the key to being free.

-Sara Tendulkar

5. The Fire Of Holika

Fiery, dense and powerful.
Fire burning in a demon's eyes.
This woman is the reason for making Holi colourful,
Her story will make you rhapsodize.

Once upon a time, is how it goes like.
Prahlad was born at a demon's place,
Who didn't like him because,
Prahlad worshiped Lord Vishnu at every fireplace.

Demon father, Hiranyakashyap, ordered Holika,
"Burn that Prahlad near his beloved fireplace"
'Sure', she said, with her skill of poetica,
And off she went to give Prahlad a chase.

Holika, unaware that the boon worked only when she alone,
Had it all backfired,
And found herself in a real loud moan.

Out from the bonfire, came Lord Vishnu, preaching,
And that's how we all started, this festival, celebrating.
Till this day we lit the beautiful bonfire,
Indicating the victory of the good;
And spreading colours throughout our neighbourhood!

-Sara Tendulkar

6. Holi

The rainbow of joy,
And the colour on your cheeks,
Be it a man or a schoolboy,
Everyone has the right to annoy.

Holi is a splendid representation,
That if we don't get to see colourful rain,
We create the sensation,
Just by applying colours like insane.

The rainbow paints the sky,
And we paint the world,
Just pick up some colours, and have them on others' face, swirled.

Red for energy, orange for creativity,
Green for nature, and purple for luxury.

Oh, there they come! The people with colours,
And oh they smash some black on my face,
Well in that case,
I give them my creepy smile,
And empty my water gun on their white textile!

-Sara Tendulkar

7. Halcyon

'Tweet, tweet' it comes, my beautiful little bird.
My heart communicates with them without using a word.

My eyes understand what that little thing means,
Oh and this time Bella came flying all the way from Philipinnes.

I sit with my birds, trees, animals near the ocean,
And all my heart does is beat melodiously,
With every wave that comes piously.
We say 'hello' to the dolphins,
And bid bye to our sins.

I count stars with Bella in the night,
Bella looks at the moon,
And takes a beautiful flight.
I see her circling in the sky and again my heart plays a beautiful

tune.

'I'm fragranted with your love' I tell Bella.
She somehow brings me the essence of vanilla.
She comes and sits again on my head,
And turns all the silence dead.

Now you'd ask me why I belong here,
Ask it to my heart, 'cause it gave that start.
It's beats always sounded strange.
So I found myself change.

It all happened on one fine day,
When I was told by a psycho,
That something fishy was on its way.
I saw a dragon in the cloud,
And that's when my heart spoke,
"You don't belong to the crowd"

I came hunting for adventures,
About which I had such strong indentures.
My heart taught me how to dream.

IRIDESCENT

It forced me to chase it,
And pushed me even when tired was every cell in my bloodstream.
It's because of the beautiful talks,
I have with my heart,
That I grew up to love nature,
The way it was!

-Sara Tendulkar

8. Story Of Every Politician

There was once a politician,
Who had a great ambition,
And had taken part in an immense competition.

"Just one vote, just one vote,
Make me win, god,
I'll stuff all modaks down your throat,
'Cause I want it to be me and my squad.

"We'll take all the money and grow richer day by day,
'Cause that's exactly why you become a politician,
To fight and create drama all the way."

"I'll frame your beautiful photo,

And give you red flowers and all,
Just make me win, god,
'Cause I want it to be me and my squad.

"Ah, the beautiful black money,
And the power I get,
In the middle of the city,
I'll have my own big statuette!"

"I'll go abroad,
Along with my tripod,
To record my drama, not on a selfie stick, but on a golden rod.
Make me win, please god,
'Cause I want it to be me and my squad!"

"My car will be twice bigger than that of Sharma ji,
me and my friends will loot all paise and every rupee."

How had this started? Oh that was simple,
Once this politician was made the class monitor which gave him this twinkle.

And oh, the elections took place,
And this one won,
'Cause maybe he worshiped god at every fireplace.

"I have the power,
Look what I do.
I'll start a matter,
And put them through.
First, I'll open instagram, twitter,
And I'll post a roast on the other party,
Which acts like Hitler.

'Oh I'll win your heart,
I'll set it on fire.
I know, I'm smart,
All you do is sit and admire.

"So the next law I'm releasing,
Sorry I won't be discussing or debating,
Because it's very sensible,
As all the people have to do is have it double.
Double what?
Their unnecessary and unvalid whatsapp forwards,
To cause panic about the virus,

And scream and run here, there and backwards.
Next, every single serial has to add dhoom tananana,
And I'm gonna check if you have the dramatic staircase fall of grandma.
All these laws are very very importan-

"Oh that law doesn't make any sense,
You need to run up the sections and find some directions"

"No no never. I know what I'm doing,
It is so valid, that it doesn't need any more viewing"

"I'm sitting in opposition,
And anyone can tell you've made a stupid decision.
I'll fight on a Sunday,
A Monday and a Tuesday.
I'll fight all the misery,
I'll fight all the wrong"

"Shut up you idiot, I'll anyways add dhoom tanana in every song"

"You dare do that, there's no damn need,
I'll fight against this law, even if I have myself bleed!"

"This is a very dumb matter to fight on
But it's okay, I'll get money, so go on"

"Be serious you dumb politician!"
Then suddenly ,suddenly that law got passed,
And every single movie,
Be it action, sad or peaceful
That dramatic song had been broadcast.
The politician earned in lakhs and crores,
For the dumbest thing he had in his brain's store.
And that's how works politics,
And if you wanna intermix,
You'll have to go through a bag of tricks.

-Sara Tendulkar

9. What Am I Related To?

I'm related to a mystery,
I'm related to words,
I can play with the story,
If I hate it, I can make it one-thirds.

Sometimes it's the words,
Who entertain me.
Just like the waves,
Which synchronize with the sea.

When I don't have anything to talk,
The voice in my mind,
Has my heart block.
Then I'm forced to tell a story
'Cause the words say it's mandatory.

Sometimes it comes right from my mouth,
Or sometimes I have to write them down with a pen.
But I make sure I go writing to the page's south,

Scratching the unnecessary ones, over and over again.

These bonds are unbreakable,
haha how can words be dead?
Friendship? Oh, this one's unbeatable.
These small things are like creatures,
Which can never leave my head.

They can take the form of a fire-breathing animal,
Money in front of them looks less valuable.
They are the ones you're proud to read,
And words are the only creatures I know I need!

-Sara Tendulkar

10. When I Said The Wrong 'Happy Birthday'

"Sim Tala bim, Shazam, Shazam,
Sim Tala bim, pollyannaism"

"Ah what did you say?"
He scratched his head.

"Oh don't you understand
It's a Japanese happy birthday"

"No wait,' someone from his side said,
"You just said some words,
Which weren't supposed to be said"

So it all started there.
Those words with which I had to bear,
Had whispered in my ears to beware.

SARA TENDULKAR

Lighting suddenly struck out of nowhere.

"Welcome dear boy, you look like the perfect toy.
I hope you're ready for level one,
Three, two, one let's have some fun"

I was thrown into a pit,
And the torches were lit.

"You look so thin, toy, do you fight at all?"
"I guess he's so dumb that he loves to fall"

They gave me no knife, they gave me no gun
They released a monster,
And all I could do was run.
The monster had saliva, trickling down his lips
He smelt so strongly of fish and chips.
His eyeballs were on fire,
I hated his attire,
His face was all black,
And he made his attack.

IRIDESCENT

I ran right and left,
Thinking of the words which I had said
God had you placed me on your cleft,
For the words which were supposed to remain unsaid.

Then was another monster released,
My stamina had decreased.
I stopped right there.
Jumped on the monster
And tore his underwear.
I climbed to his head
And plucked his horn
I smashed it in his eye instead
And stole the fireball.
I set fire everywhere
With that stupid red eyeball.
And I dropped back on my bed,
I had won the battle and the monster was dead.

-Sara Tendulkar

11. Unlock That Cage

Why to keep a dream in a cage,
Let it go perform on a stage.
Dream of clouds,
Dream of skies,
There would be crowds,
Giving your stomach butterflies.

I have the fear of stage,
And I'm locked in its cage,
But I know someday,
I'll do it like a child's play.

I'll hold my mic,
And start it out loud,
The cage will be on strike,
And I'd be on the ninth cloud.

I know why a caged bird sings,
Because it thinks it can't spread it wings,

IRIDESCENT

It anyways covers the sky,
By singing melodiously,
And without having to fly.

-Sara Tendulkar

12. Hill He'd Always Wanted To Climb

'No don't catch him, let him fall'
Let him respond to the skill's call.
He tells me that he had suffocated his lungs with joy,
So it was his responsibility to try and try.

He picked up the brush, and started it again,
Mistakes over mistakes, gave him pain.
Sweat from his forehead,
Dripped on the page,
But still he kept trying, 'cause he wanted to take over the stage.

Another wrong stroke, and the portrait looked like a mountain,
In the drawing, her face was ruined, her hair was messed like a fountain.
He picked up the drawing and tore it all,
'Cause he knew very well, this was his hundredth fall.

IRIDESCENT

The model laughed at him,
No, he wasn't losing his hope,
He made the drop of water swim,
On the patch in which he found scope.

Stroke to the left, and stroke to the right,
This time he was glued to his painting real tight.
He dipped the brush in and took the last drop of paint,
This was his final stroke,
Which made the lady faint.

She widened her eyes when he turned around her portrait,
She rushed to her bag and lent him extra money from her wallet.
'Boy, this is a masterpiece'
She exclaimed with tears,
The boy was glad that he had faced his fears.

'You've got that skill'
Said his teacher from behind,
'Now you need to climb that hill,

'Cause now you have more things to find!'

-Sara Tendulkar

13. The Real Kind Of Adventures

Stars in my favorite constellation,
Were smiling at me,
As I walked towards my destination
On a really dark night, along the sea.

Oh I'll tell you,
About those waves, and ah, their sound,
As they hit the rocks,
Went back and drowned.
And when the waves sat still,
They reflected the moonshine,
Which gave my heart that wonderful thrill,
As I looked past the coastline.
The wind interrupted me and reminded me of my adventure,
I said 'oh' and left the beautiful picture.

Of all the cities I saw,
This was the most bright one,

Then suddenly came a paw,
And ruined my fun.

Very ugly ,very dark,
But no,it didn't look like a shark.
It took away my map,
And tore it in his lap.
This happened in a snap,
That I failed to get him in a trap.

It came at my sack,
But I pulled out my knife,
I tried to stab his back,
As I had been taught by my wife.

It looked at me,
And didn't do anything.
It really didn't mind me,
It was kinda upto something.

IRIDESCENT

The little black thing,
slowly pushed down my knife.
I tell you it was upto something,
But I couldn't wait and sacrifice my life.

It suddenly started talking,
And told me to get lost.
I became furious,
And had my limits crossed.

I stabbed it in its back,
My very own knife,
And ran to my sack,
As I realized it lost its life.

Its eyes lay motionless,
Its ugly fur lay still,
I felt a bit hopeless,
And slowly died my thrill.

The ugly black animal,
Had left in my sack a note,
It was titled 'valuable'

SARA TENDULKAR

So I couldn't emote.

I opened it fast,
And read out those words,
'Dear mister adventurer,
You may think I'm a creepy creature,
But I've got something beautiful to tell you,
Burn your maps and follow your heart,
Explore the world, a work of art.
Not with a map, not with a compass,
Not with your bag, please throw away that hourglass.
This could be your adventure of a lifetime,
Don't keep a destination,
Just wander off,
And let your footsteps rhyme.
Keep going wherever your mind wanders
And the next destination,
Could be you entering your imagination?'

I really started crying when I realized my crime,
What an irony was this creature whom I had encountered on this dark night.
It had taught me a lesson,
To not be ordinary,
I threw away my weapon,

IRIDESCENT

'Cause it was so necessary.
I buried the little thing near the seashore,
Along with my compass, my tears and one thing more.

The creature was my inspiration,
Better than that constellation,
So without any destination,
On that dark night,
For this beautiful creature,
I set off on my adventure.

-Sara Tendulkar

14. Work Like Crazy

How about making the ordinary come alive?
And that too in two, three, four and five.
No, it's not like that, my dear,
First things first, you'll need to face your fear.

You'll need to do the things you've never done before,
And keep doing them until they aren't left anymore.
These '5 a.m's can make you a star,
Work harder, and let others say that you're bizarre.

Get up when you fall,
If you're tired, I don't care,
'Cause you'll get nothing or all,
It's all upto you, if you wanna get there.

It's a slow journey,
I pretty much agree,
But soon you'll be free,
Just fall in love with the process, you see.

IRIDESCENT

-Sara Tendulkar

15. Watchout! There's Smoke Coming Out Of Your Eyes

You seriously need to thank god,
For he has given you that flame in your eyes,
And you'll start to applaud,
When you realize how fast it can burn a big cube of ice.

This flame is full of passion,
And it can't be extinguished,
It will force you to get to action,
'Cause our aim is to not get relinquished.

Trust me, this unstoppable flame,
Will show you your potential,
You may lose or win the game,
But you'll learn, 'cause that's essential.

IRIDESCENT

You wouldn't need a song for motivation,
You wouldn't need anyone to push you to work,
Because you've mastered the art to get over your procrastination,
You very well know your framework.

Let your eyes smoke,
And make yourself look bizarre,
You'll soon make your stroke,
And your dream will make you a star.

-Sara Tendulkar

16. Wild Little Storm

How cool would it be,
If you be the storm yourself,
You can fly over the sea,
And scare the sailors sipping tea.

You can breathe in the rain,
And breathe it out like a tornado,
It will keep growing insane,
And you can enjoy it from your meadow.

You can play with the demons,
You can play with the weather,
You can mess up the news channels,
And take it even more farther.

How about moving the moon?
And carrom with the stars?
You can blow up a balloon,

IRIDESCENT

Maybe till Mars.

You don't need to worry about withstanding the storm,
Because storm is how you were born.

-Sara Tendulkar

17. Paper Boats

Have you wondered,
Where our small paper boats go?
We think they are just boats colored,
Which move within our blow.

But no, that's all a big fat lie,
The boats sail and sail,
Until the sixth of July,
They go through the storm, they go through the hail,
But they make it to the sea,
That we all know as 'Cocktail'

There they turn into small toy ships,
With a captain and a crew,
Eating fish and chips.

Hundred more boats come,
Oh, the number can go upto thousand,
Each boat turns into a different color,

IRIDESCENT

Some into pear and some into plum.

They go on adventures,
To find chests full of treasures,
Oh how I wish I could be one of them,
I could sail on the ships at 10 p.m.

-Sara Tendulkar

18. Unity

One pencil working alone,
Can write a book in one year.
But when it comes to blood and stone,
Five pencils say 'hold our beer'.
Pencil number one scratches the page,
While the others start dancing.
Unity silently steps on the stage,
And the book's born right before spring.
Unity is magic,
'Cause it weaves everything into one piece of fabric.

-Sara Tendulkar

19. The Sky Full Of Words

What if, instead of reading through books,
We looked up and read through skies?
Skies decorated with words like brooks,
Fullstops would be those butterflies.

I would lay down on the grass,
And yell the name of what I want to read,
From the air, a leaf would surpass,
And on the sky would be the words I need.

Then I wouldn't even mind the sunburn,
I wouldn't even mind who's dead,
I'll be engrossed in the story's twist and turn,
If you disturb me, I'll hit you with a French bread.

When it would be night,
The stars would twinkle,
Words would turn white,
Ah, that's better than kindle.

SARA TENDULKAR

The words would arrange themselves,
According to the constellations.
When I'd reach the last word,
They'll display 'congratulations'.

-Sara Tendulkar

www.ingramcontent.com/pod-product-compliance
Lightning Source LLC
LaVergne TN
LVHW041548060526
838200LV00037B/1202